Why Didn't Noah Swat Both Mosquitoes?

Plus Other Humorous Stories For Clergy

Hoover Rupert

CSS Publishing Company, Inc.
Lima, Ohio

Copyright © 1994 by
The CSS Publishing Company, Inc.
Lima, Ohio

Library of Congress Cataloging-in-Publication Data

Rupert, Hoover.
    Why didn't Noah swat both mosquitoes? : plus other humorous stories for preaching / Hoover Rupert.
        p.   cm.
    Includes index.
    1. Homiletical illustrations. 2. American wit and humor. 3. Christian life—Humor. 4. Christian life—Anecdotes. I. Title.
BV4225.2.RF   1994
251'.08——dc20   93-44439
                                                                CIP

ISBN 1-55673-519-7   PRINTED IN U.S.A.

This Is For

TOM MATHENY

Strong Churchman
Noted Raconteur
Good Friend

Table Of Contents

Introduction

Someone has said there are less than 10 basic jokes and that all others are simply variations on one or more of these. Certainly you have heard the same story in different settings many times. So much of our humor is transmitted by word of mouth that it is a well-nigh impossible task to find the original source for most stories you hear. Recall the most recent funny story you have heard. Now, can you tell me who or what is the original source of that story?

Believe me, after two solid years of trying to trace some 2,500 stories in my files to their original sources, I can testify that it is a tedious and most difficult task.

It is most interesting to read in a periodical of current date a joke or story which I was telling 30 or 40 years ago. And quite often no printed source is given. Except for a relatively few stories that have been in the public domain — usage for at least 30 years — every one of the stories herein has an acknowledged source. If the story is original with me or one which I have been telling for 40 to 50 years, I have placed my initials H.R. following it. In addition, where my files indicated where and when I heard the story, I have included that information. The many stories credited to my father, Rev. Lynn H. Rupert, now deceased, are among the hundreds I heard him tell across the years of his ministry.

As an aid to your use of this resource, I have provided an alphabetized index in the back of the book.

Many book and periodical publishers granted permission to use copyrighted material. I have made an honest effort to trace every item to a source.

A Final Word

Since I am a preacher who has made generous use of illustrative humor for more than 50 years, it may be assumed that the stories herein are exclusively for the clergy. Such is not the case. To be sure, I originally designed the anthology for the busy preacher who needs a humorous illustration for Sunday's sermon, or the next civic club address, or to enhance one's reputation as a raconteur, or even to display occasionally a sense of humor. However, I shared the manuscript with several laypersons who speak publicly with regularity and they all found it to be helpful to them as well. They have encouraged me to believe that any public speaker will find stories, anecdotes, definitions, put downs, stories from and about kids, and one-liners, which can be used with good results.

Just remember, they may not long remember the profundity of the truth of your message, but they will remember the story, which illustrates it. That memory could remind them of the truth as well.

Some of the stories here you have doubtless heard and perhaps have told. But I believe you will find enough "new" material organized for quick reference, so that you are justified in adding this book to your resource library.

Following each individual item, you will find the name of the publication and/or the name of the person which/whom is my source for that item. Details concerning copyright and permissions or individual sources are to be found in the acknowledgment pages.

Hoover Rupert
Gaithersburg, Maryland

A

Accidents

Rodney Wilmoth recalls an experience several years ago when he was the United Methodist pastor in Fremont, Nebraska. A staff member came to work one morning saying that the others there would never believe what had happened to one of her neighbors on her street. Apparently the day before this man had climbed up on the roof of his house to do some minor repairs.

Because of the steep pitch of the roof, he decided to tie a rope around his waist and then throw the rope over the top of the house down to the other side of the house so it would reach the ground. At that point, he called for his son and told him to tie the end of the rope to something secure. The boy tied the rope to the bumper of the car, which was in the driveway. It seemed to work well and the man proceeded with his work feeling the greatest sense of security.

Then his wife, who was unaware of her husband's ingenious security measure, decided to run an errand which required the use of the car. She did not see the rope tied to the bumper, and pulled out of the driveway. You know the result. The man survived, but Dr. Wilmoth reports that in hearing her tell the story he pictured this man soaring over the peak of that roof like Evel Knievel over the Snake River Canyon.

Rodney Wilmoth

Actors

A student was called on to say one line in a public school play. He was to come in and say, "Fear not; it is I." In the excitement of the moment and frightened as he was, the old habits of speech rose up. He blurted out in an excited manner, "Don't be scared — ain't nobody but me!"

Wilson Weldon

Aged

When Bishop Welch was 100 years old, hundreds of his friends gathered at the Waldorf Astoria to pay tribute to his life. Abingdon Press had just published his book, *My First Hundred Years*. As part of the program, book editor Emory Bucke presented the bishop with the first copy of the book. He facetiously suggested that he hoped Bishop Welch would still be around in 50 years so Abingdon could publish a sequel autobiography. Bishop Welch's comment to Bucke, who was then 50, was this: "Emory, I'll be here. I just hope you will be. More people who are now 50 will die in the next 50 years than those who are now 100, so I really have a better chance of being here than you do.

A church publication news item.

Agreement

Here's to the man who is wisest and best
Here's to the man who with judgment is blest,
Here's to the man who's as smart as can be —
I mean the man who agrees with me.

Author unknown

Animals

A motorist was driving in the country when his car stopped suddenly. He got out and was checking the spark plugs when an old horse came trotting up the road. "Better check the carburetor," said the horse and trotted on. The motorist ran to the nearest farmhouse and told the farmer what had happened.

"Was it a brown horse with a flopping ear?" asked the farmer.

"Yes! Yes!" cried the man.

"Well, sir," said the farmer, "don't pay any attention to him. He doesn't know anything about cars."

The Lion

B

Babies

The inquisitive neighbor approached the expectant mother in her back yard and asked her point blank: "Are you going to have a baby?"

The young woman smiled sweetly and replied, "Oh, goodness, no. I'm merely carrying this for a friend."

F. G. Kernan, Quote

It was their first child. The husband was at work when he got word that his wife had driven from home to the hospital and that the big event was expected momentarily. He rushed to the hospital and arrived just as they were wheeling his wife back to her room.

"Is everything all right?" he asked.

"I don't know," she said anxiously. "Run out and check the car quick. I had to park in a two-hour zone."

Quote

Baldness

God made a few perfect heads, the rest he covered with hair.

A preacher in West Virgina was calling on a rural home. The man of the house was bald-headed as was the preacher. The farmer said, "It won't be long, Parson, before you have to tie a string around your head to tell how far up to wash your face."

Leewin B. Williams

12

Banking

A package of $100 bills was missing at the bank. The staff worked all night trying to locate them. Next morning, Sally, a new clerk walked into the bank to begin her daily duties.

An officer of the bank asked her, "Sally, did you see a package of $100 bills?"

"Oh that," said Sally. "Why, I just took them home to show mother the kind of work I'm doing."

Grit

There was a janitor in a big city bank who was sweeping up the floor of the president's office after banking hours. A telephone rang and he answered it. The excited voice at the other end of the line demanded, "I want to know what the Federal Reserve Bank discount is, what the prime-paper rate is, and if all this foreign travel is going to upset our currency." "Mister," the janitor replied, "I told you all I know about banking when I said hello."

Gerald Kennedy, Fresh Every Morning

Banquets

What is a banquet? It is an affair where persons all dressed-up gather among comparative strangers, pay an astronomical price to eat cold meat and potatoes, and tasteless broccoli, topped off by melting ice cream. Then the speaker, who has eaten a lot of food he didn't want, proceeds to talk a long time about something he doesn't understand, to a lot of people who don't really want to hear him, and then collects a big fee for his effort.

Adapted from Leewin B. Williams

Will Rogers was a veteran of the creamed chicken circuit. He once said that he had spoken at so many banquets during a given year that when he got home, he felt disappointed if his wife or one of the children didn't get up at dinner and say, "We have with us this evening, a man who, I am sure, needs no introduction."

One speaker at a banquet was very warmly received by the audience because he stood up when introduced and said, "I am here speaking to you tonight because I don't have anything else to do. And, I am sitting down because I have nothing else to say."

When they threw Daniel in the lions' den, his first thought as he looked at the hungry beasts was, "At least I won't have to make an after-dinner speech."

H.R.

Two orators of a previous generation were Joseph Choate and Chauncey M. Depew. Ambassador Choate was the speaker at a dinner and he was to be introduced by Senator Depew. Depew said, "Gentlemen, permit me to introduce Ambassador Choate, America's most inveterate after-dinner speaker. All you need to do to get a speech out of Mr. Choate is to open his mouth, drop in a dinner and up comes your speech."

The Ambassador arose, thanked the Senator for his compliment, and then said, "Mr. Depew said if I open my mouth and drop in a dinner up will come a speech. But, I warn you if you open up your mouth and drop one of Senator Depew's speeches, up will come your dinners."

Leewin B. Williams

Baptism

The gambler had been converted in a revival meeting and was being baptized in the river. As he was put under the water, five playing cards (including four aces) slipped out of his sleeve or pocket and floated momentarily on the river. The preacher wondered out loud if the conversion was genuine. A friend on the bank called out, "Don't worry about him, Preacher, with a hand like that he can't lose!"

Heard in the 1940s

A child had watched her first baptism and heard the words, "In the name of the Father and the Son and the Holy Ghost." She and a friend were playing baptism in the back yard. She baptized her doll "In the name of the Father and the Son and the Holy Go."

1950s

Another backyard baptism was for a kitten. The kids had dug a hole big enough for the kitten, and filled it with water. Then one of them pronounced the words: "In the name of the Father and the Son and in-the-hole-he-goes."

H.R.

Back in the 1930s, during the dust storms and drought, there was a report circulating in Kansas that it had been so long since the last rain that the Baptists were "sprinkling," the Methodists were "dry cleaning" and the Presbyterians were giving out rain checks.

H.R.

A Baptist preacher was candidating for a small church in the south. He preached his trial sermon on water baptism — baptism by immersion — and pointed out how this was the only biblically acceptable form of baptism. He preached well and the congregation agreed with his convictions on the matter. So they called him a pastor.

15

The first Sunday there he preached on water baptism. This was all right with them because he introduced some new slants on the same subject. Second Sunday — same theme. After the third Sunday of "water baptism," the deacons waited on the pastor and the chairman said, "We believe what you believe about water baptism. But isn't there some other theme you could preach on?" He asked for suggestions. One deacon asked why he didn't preach on the books of the Bible — "one each Sunday, that could occupy a whole year or more."

So, the next Sunday he announced to the congregation that at the suggestion of the deacons he would be preaching on the successive books of the Bible. "Today I am preaching on Genesis. It says, 'In the beginning God created the heavens and the earth.' Then he swung the stars into place in the heavens and on earth created seven seas, which brings us to the subject of water baptism —."

Heard at a district conference in 1940

Baptists

Some years ago I was speaking in Columbia, South Carolina, at a state-wide Youth Day. The morning session was at the Washington Street Methodist Church. The evening session was at the First Baptist Church which seated 1,500, considerably more than the other church, and it was filled. As I sat on the platform in the ante-bellum church built in the early 1800s, the chairman told me that I would be standing as I spoke, on the spot where the papers of secession for South Carolina were signed in 1861, leading to the Civil War.

Later I learned that when General Sherman came to Columbia, he was determined to burn down the Baptist Church because of the signing of the secession papers. When the squad of soldiers arrived at the front of the church, the janitor met them and asked what they were going to do. "Burn down this church," said the lieutenant, "because this is where those rebs signed that secession paper and the general wants it burned to the ground."

16

The janitor said, "No, sir, you have the wrong church. It is that church down the block there," and pointed to the Washington Street Church. So the squad marched down the block and actually burned the Methodist Church. Its present building shows 1869 as the construction date, and the antebellum First Baptist Church still stands where it did.

H.R.

The late congressman Brooks Hayes was a former president of the Southern Baptist Convention. He said he made the mistake of paraphrasing in front of his wife: "The Lord must like us Southern Baptists — he made so many of us."

"Oh, yeah!" replied 90-pound Mrs. Hayes, a Methodist. "He's just trying to find a good one."

In a public address

Bible

The Sunday school teacher had just finished a detailed account of Jonah and the whale. "And now Willie, can you tell us what lesson this story teaches?" she asked one of the boys.

"Yes'm," said Willie. "It teaches that you can't keep a good man down."

Herb Walker

Stockbroker to minister: "As a financier, you could say Noah was really underrated. He floated his stock while all others were being liquidated."

In another class, the teacher asked how Noah spent his time on the ark. One kid replied that Noah must have done a lot of fishing. But another youngster scoffed, "What, with only two worms?"

The teacher was telling the children's class about the story of Lot. "Lot was warned to take his wife and flee out of the city, but his wife looked back and was turned to salt. Any questions?"

"Yes," said one little girl, "I was wondering what happened to his flea."

Quote

The topic was Elijah and the prophets of Baal on Mt. Carmel. The teacher explained that he built an altar, placed wood upon it, cut the sacrificial bullock in pieces, and laid them on the wood. He then commanded the people to fill four jars with water and pour the water over the sacrifice. "Why do you think they did that?" she asked. A little girl raised her hand and said, "To make gravy."

A man was marooned in a small mountain town because of a landslide caused by heavy rain. Rain was still falling in torrents after three days. Pointing to the rain, he remarked to the waitress, "This is like the great flood."

"The what?" asked the waitress.

"You know, the great flood. Surely you have heard of the great flood and Noah and the Ark."

"No, Mister," she replied, "I haven't seen a newspaper in four days."

One little boy had wisdom in his jumbled version of a Bible verse from the Old Testament, "A lie is an abomination unto the Lord, and a very present help in trouble."

Thomas L. Butts

An adult class teacher was pointing out how relatively small Palestine is by pointing on the map to Dan and Beersheba.

18

A man in the class interrupted at this point to exclaim, "Do you mean Dan and Beersheba were places? I always thought they were brother and sister like Sodom and Gomorrah."

First heard in 1945

The boys in the class listened intently as the teacher told the parable of the prodigal son. After emphasizing the disagreeable attitude of the older brother, she described the rejoicing in the household at the return of the wandering son.

Then she said, "In the midst of this celebration, however, there was one who failed to share in the festive spirit. Now, does anyone know who that was?"

Waving a hand frantically, one small boy said, "The fatted calf."

Lynn H. Rupert

There is a story about a preacher who started to read the Bible in the service without knowing that some youngsters had prankishly glued two pages together. So he read from the bottom of one page, "When Noah was 120 years old he took unto himself a wife, who was —" and here he turned the glued pages and continued — "140 cubits long, 40 cubits wide, built of gopher wood, and covered with pitch inside and out." He stopped; he read the passage again. Obviously he was puzzled. But he finally said, "I don't ever remember reading that in the Bible before, but I accept it as evidence that we are fearfully and wonderfully made."

From one of many versions

A nine-year-old youngster was the only one in his Sunday school class who responded when the teacher asked who knew the story of Jonah. After his accurate summary, the teacher complimented him on being the only student in the class who read the Bible lesson that week.

19

Painfully honest, the boy corrected the teacher. "I didn't read it in the Bible," he explained. "It was on a bubble gum wrapper."

Cappers

The Sunday school teacher was talking about the Sermon on the Mount. "Where do you find the Beatitudes?" she asked. There was a long silence until one child piped up: "In the Yellow Pages?"

Detroit Free Press

Two Methodists were trying to best each other in their knowledge of the church, the Bible, and faith. One man said to the other, "Why, I'll bet you ten dollars you can't even recite the Lord's Prayer."

The other man said, "It's a bet." Then he said, "Now I lay me down to sleep. I pray the Lord my soul to keep." The other man said. "Here's your ten dollars. I didn't think you could do it."

Mark Trotter

Reading a sentence in a novel which told of a woman crossing the street in a wheelchair, against the traffic light, and opining that she "probably would have whizzed past the burning bush," led me to ask some biblical questions:

•Suppose Moses had been tending sheep in a golf cart, would he have whizzed past the burning bush?

•Where would John the Baptist have been preaching if he had graduated from college and seminary? Probably First Church, Jerusalem.

•Suppose Jericho Light and Power Co. had cut down that sycamore tree the day before Jesus came to Jericho. Would we have heard of Zacchaeus?

•What a blessing it would have been, if Noah had swatted those two mosquitoes!

20

•What if Joshua couldn't find any clay pitchers before the siege of Jericho?

•Whatever happened to the Golden Calf?

•How could Daniel have demonstrated his faith, if the lions had been toothless?

•What color suit would Adam have purchased, if Brooks Brothers had had a branch store in Eden?

•If Jonah had covered himself with tar and rolled in the sand, would the whale have swallowed him?

•What if Eli had given Samuel a sleeping pill the first time he woke up the old priest?

•What if Joseph had discovered a gold mine in that pit?

•Is it true that when Eve asked Adam if he were seeing another woman, he replied, "Who else?"

•Couldn't his friends have built a chute for the cripple at Bethesda?

H.R.

At a Sunday school convention, four so-called "biblical preachers" had been invited to preach on dancing. It happened that each used the same text from 2 Samuel, "And David danced before the Ark." The first preacher suggested that this was simply a reference to a kind of religious processional used as the people entered the place of worship. Therefore, this was no biblical sanction to dance.

The second said the text had an implied verb which said David danced before the Ark danced, and had nothing to do with the current curse of ballroom dancing.

The third said it was a time factor. David danced before the Ark was placed in the temple, but there was no record he ever danced again — therefore, dancing had to be biblically outlawed.

But, the last preacher was a bit more liberal. He said that young people can dance if they wish, because it is very clear that David had no compunctions about dancing — even in the presence of the Lord!

Heard at pastor's school

The Methodist Council of Bishops met in Los Angeles about the time Cecile B. DeMille's epic film, *The Ten Commandments*, was to be released. Mr. DeMille spoke to the Council about it, and then showed a preview. He told the story which has had wide circulation since. It's about the girl who came home from Sunday school to report that the lesson was on the escape of the Children of Israel from Egypt. She told of how Moses erected a pontoon bridge across the Red Sea. Then he called in his airplane bombers and destroyed the bridge just as Pharaoh's army was in the middle of it. Her mother suggested that this could hardly be true in that ancient day, and asked why the girl had embroidered the story so. "Well, Mother," she replied, "if I had told you the story the way our teacher told it, you would never have believed it."

Heard this from one who was there

Some biblical corn:
The first boy mentioned in the Bible was Chap. One.
The first girl mentioned in the Bible was Jenny's Sis.
Tennis came in when David served in Pharaoh's court.
Baseball is referred to in the Prodigal's home run, and when
    Samson made a hit with the jaw bone of an ass.
Cars are mentioned when Ahab came raging from the Ford.
Russian noblemen included Baron Figtree, Lord Howlong, and
    County Not-the-Cost-Thereof.
Goliath was slain by the axe of the apostles.
The epistles were the wives of the apostles.

The final of the Bible stories comes from the farewell dinner given our family when we left Jackson, Michigan, for Ann Arbor. Gifts were presented to each one of our daughters. Eight-year-old Elizabeth was given a white Bible with gold engraving. It was presented to her unwrapped, as she and Sarah, her presenting little friend, stood at the microphone before 650 diners. Elizabeth saw her name in gold on the Bible cover, and gasped, "Oh, thank you so much. I've never had a Bible."

H.R.

22

Bragging

Bragging may not bring happiness, but did you ever see a man, having caught a large fish, go home through an alley?"

The Lion

The man was reading the schedule for his lodge's upcoming meetings. He snorted about one program, "He's going to talk to us about his naval experiences? Poppycock! The nearest he ever came to a naval experience was when his basement flooded and his rowing machine sank."

A friend of Barry Bailey was sick for quite some time but reported that you really can't win because there is always someone around who has been sicker than you. Someone told this friend, "You had it easy. You were in the marvelous All Saints' Hospital with the best care. When I was sick, I was in a hospital so far away from modern science that in order to have an X-ray, they held me up before an open window."

Barry Bailey

Bumper Stickers

While there are many bumper stickers appearing today which are vulgar, suggestive and profane, there are some that are clean and still good for a laugh. Here are a few I have collected:
"SO R U."
"If you are rich, I'm single."
"God said it. I believe it. That settles it!"
"Let's not meet by accident."
"I'm not deaf. I'm ignoring you."
"I owe, I owe, so it's off to work I go."

"Beam me up, Scotty, there is no intelligent life down here."
"Mom's taxi service."
"If you can read this, you are too close."
"My other car is a Rolls."
"Don't laugh. It's paid for. Is yours?"
"When God created man, she was only joking."
"Women like the simple things in life — men."
"They found something that does the work of six men — one woman."
"Pass with care, driver chews tobacco."
"I hate slow cars in the fast lane."
"Go ahead and hit me. I need the money."
"I may be slow, but I'm ahead of you."
"As a matter of fact, I do own the road."
"The more I know men, the more I love my cat."
"Trust in God. She will provide."
"If you think I drive bad, you should see me putt."
"I never get lost — People tell me where to go."
"Become a doctor and support a lawyer."
"You're not much if you're not Dutch."
"Everybody is entitled to my opinion."
"Forget the whales. Save me!"
"Mafia Mutual: You hit us — we hit you."
"Get really stoned — Drink wet concrete."
"On a quiet night you can hear a Ford rust" (IN DETROIT)

H.R.

Bureaucracy

Leo Aikman reports that when the Lord told Moses he was to lead the Children of Israel out of Egypt, he said, "Moses, I have some good news and some bad news for you. The good news is that you will divide the waters of the Red Sea. The bad news is that before you do you'll have to file an Environmental Impact Statement."

Atlanta Constitution

C

Camel

Three camels tried to get on board Noah's Ark. He stopped them and said only two of them could enter.

"It won't be me," said the first camel. "I'm the camel whose back is broken by the last straw."

"I'm the one people swallow while straining at a gnat," said the second.

"I," said the third, "am the one that shall pass through the eye of a needle sooner than a rich man shall enter heaven."

"Come on in," said Noah. "The world is going to need all three of you."

Clergy Talk

Campus And College Students

A professor in a class on religion was trying to explain the difference between fact and faith. He said, "You and the rest of the students in this room are sitting here before me in these seats. That is a fact. It is a fact that I am now speaking to you from this podium. It is, however, only faith that makes me believe that any of you are listening to what I am saying."

Herb Walker

This probably belongs in this college section as much as anywhere. There is an old Armenian axion which says, "If you cannot find a solution, change the problem."

A University of Texas student once reported that a restroom had a hot-air hand-drying machine on the wall. Someone had taped a sign next to the starter button which read, "For a short lecture by the Dean, push button."

25

Willis Tate, late president of SMU told of a letter he received from the mother of an entering freshman. She asked that special care be given to the selection of her son's roommate, particularly with respect to drinking, smoking, and profanity. She explained her concern in these words, "You see, Dr. Tate, my son has never been away from home except for his two years in the Marines."

Cemetery

The village council had a proposal to build a wall around the town cemetery. Arguments were loud and strong pro and con. The proposers said it would dress up the place and make it more attractive. The telling opposition argument came from an old timer who said, "Why build a wall? Nobody out wants in and nobody in wants out!"

Lynn H. Rupert

Children's Sermons

The pastor of a church gave a brief children's sermon. In the middle of his comments, a little boy raised his hand and asked, "Do you wear anything under your robe?" (The robe is a neck-to-floor white robe, zipped shut.) Reminds you of the perennial question of the Scotsman who wears kilts!

H.R.

Christmas

Melvin Wheatley tells a story about a man who kept his car in a downtown garage that daily picked up from and delivered to his office building. Early in Advent season, on the front seat of his car, he found a card that read, "Merry Christmas from the Boys at the Garage."

He had every intent of sending the manager of the garage a yuletide check to be divided among "the boys," but somehow he was delayed in doing so. Several days later he found another card on the front seat. This one said, "Merry Christmas from the Boys at the Garage — Second Notice."

Mel Wheatley

Ray Balcomb told of receiving a Christmas cartoon some years ago. It showed Mary riding a donkey, Joseph leading: in the distance was Bethlehem under a giant star. And Mary was saying, "It's Christmas, I'm pregnant, God knows how, and now you tell me you forgot to book a room! Terrific!"

Ray Balcomb

The preacher enlisted the help of four children with his Christmas sermon on "The Star." Each child had a lettered card of the word "star." They were to stand before the congregation with the four cards while the preacher preached.

They looked fine with their backs to the congregation. When they turned around, they were in reverse order and spelled out RATS.

H.R.

A Long Island commuter into New York was asked by his pastor to order a sign for the church yard for the Christmas season from an in-town sign company. The man forgot the message and dimensions and wired the pastor for the information. The telegraph operator at the Western Union fainted after typing the return message which was, "Unto us a child is born six feet long and three feet wide."

H.R.

Church

A little boy was invited by a friend to go to his church. He explained he was not allowed to do so. When asked why, he replied, "Because I belong to a different abomination."

Or, there was a youngster who wrote his sister from summer camp:

"Dear Sister: They make you walk in a pan of chemical water every time you go in swimming. I think it's so you don't get Catholic's foot."

Donald Shelby

In a small southern church, a meeting of the board was called to discuss the proposal that they purchase a chandelier for the church. One member said they "couldn't order no chandelier because nobody here can spell it." Another said, "Even if we could spell it, we don't have the money to buy it." A third person spoke up and said, "You're both right, but if we had the money and could spell it, ain't nobody in the congregation that could play a tune on it."

The pastor finally stood up, and with great dignity and restraint, said, "All of you are right, but you know while y'all were talking, I was thinking; I was thinking that we don't need a chandelier. What this church needs is more light."

Heard at various times since 1965

A bishop had come back to his hometown in the Kentucky mountains to preside at the trial of a pastor charged with using profanity. The bishop made it clear at the outset that he could continue the trial only if there was a witness who could testify that he had actually heard the pastor swear. A man came forward to claim he had heard such. He was sworn in, and then asked the bishop, "Do you remember Sister Elviry?"

The bishop responded that he did.

"Well," said the witness, "it was at her funeral which the pastor conducted. Seems Sister Elviry had been dead for two or three days when they found her. She was all stove up with arthritis and her body was all bent over. Burying Sam did a good job on her, but he had to tie her head to the bottom of the casket with bailing wire. In the middle of the parson's funeral sermon, that wire gave way and Sister Elviry sat up in the casket."

28

The bishop interrupted to ask, "Is that when you heard the pastor use profanity?"

"No, bishop," he said. "It was 30 seconds later. I was running about a quarter of a mile from the church and the parson passed me with a window frame around his neck screaming, 'These damned one-door churches!' "

H.R.

When W.E. Sangster was pastor of Westminster Central Hall in London, the Sunday evening congregations overflowed the 3,000 seat sanctuary. In his biography of his father, Paul Sangster tells that one Sunday evening a wealthy dowager got out of her chauffeured limousine and climbed the steps to the vestibule of the sanctuary. The service had already begun and as usual the hall was packed. She demanded to be admitted. The usher graciously told her that every seat was taken and all the standees they could put in the room were there already. When she reminded him just who she was, he responded most apologetically, but said he could not let her go in.

She stormed back down the stairs and yelled at her chauffeur, "No wonder people don't attend church anymore if they get treated like this!"

Heard in London, 1962

Then there is the old one of similar nature which tells of an English church so crowded that the pastor asked the verger to stand outside with a notice reading, "House Full." A little man ran up and wanted to enter. Upon being refused admission, he pleaded that he had a very urgent message to deliver to James Jones — on a matter of life and death.

The verger, a kind old man, eventually agreed to the request. "All right," he said, "you can slip in — but heaven help you if I catch you praying."

Quote

When Bishop Arthur Moore was elected to the episcopacy, he was pastor of Travis Park Church in San Antonio. He was succeeded there by Dr. Paul B. Kern, later to become bishop also. Bishop Moore had spoken all over the south about the crowds which attended Travis Park, which was filled every Sunday morning and evening. He spoke of the thrill of preaching to 2,500 persons at each service.

Bishop Kern saw similiar crowds on Sundays, but one day he counted the seats, which were opera chairs, and there were only 1,847 seats. He sent Moore a telegram and asked how he could preach to 2,500 people in a sanctuary that seated only 1,847. Bishop Moore replied with a telegram which said, "Dear Brother Paul: you will find that you always preach to more people if you do not count them."

Told to me by Bishop Kern

An Episcopal visitor to our Epworth Heights summer pulpit told of a rector who started the ritual with "The Lord be with you." There was no response because the microphone was not on. So he said, "There's something wrong with this mike." Just then the attendant turned the PA switch and the congregation responded, "And with you also."

H.R.

A minister was perturbed over the absenteeism of some of his members. He gave his secretary a list of 10 members who were most frequently absent and asked her to write them each a letter on church stationery concerning their absences. A few days later the minister received a letter from a prominent lawyer who apologized profusely for having been absent so often. He enclosed a check for $1,000 to cover contributions he would have made had he been present. He promised to be there the following Sunday and every Sunday thereafter unless providentially hindered.

30

The minister was wondering as he read this what his secretary had written in order to get such a prompt and positive response. By the time he finished the letter he began to have some idea of how she had approached the subject. The lawyer closed the letter with a usual complimentary salutation and his signature. Then he added a note at the bottom of the page that read: "Please inform your secretary that there is only one 'T' in dirty and that there is no 'C' in skunk."

Thomas L. Butts

One of the stories I grew up with was about the church janitor who is probably one of the most harried individuals. Anyone who puts a dollar in the offering plate figures he can order the janitor around. This one had a plateful of problems that day with women's circles meetings all over the church building. One lady asked him how he could put up with so many bosses telling him what to do. He replied, "It's easy. I just throws my mind into neutral and goes where I'm pushed."

Lynn H. Rupert

Another story I have heard and told for years concerns building a new church building. The pastor insisted that nobody could see the inside of the sanctuary until the day of the opening service. He and the architect, a member of the congregation, had a surprise for the people. On the day of the first service, the people were lined up for a block. An usher came out and counted off the first 14 persons, letting them in. When they saw the inside, it was empty of pews, except for two back pews each seating seven. They were seated, they heard a motor whir and the pew moved gracefully down the nave and became the first row. Then another group, who got the same treatment, became the second row. And so on — everyone sat down in a back pew, but all the front pews were filled!

The preacher beamed all through the service — no empty front rows. But there was a surprise for him that the architect hadn't told him about. When the court house clock struck noon, a trap door just behind the pulpit opened up and the preacher disappeared!

H.R.

Communication

Gerald Kennedy reported that he was at an African Annual Conference to preach, when his host, the bishop, told him a story about a woman who had come through there shortly before. She was a worker with what was then the Women's Society of Christian Service, and had recently received her Ph.D. He said she was indeed a very bright young woman and was to preach in this same pulpit. An African, who knew fairly good English, was to be her interpreter.

She began that morning by saying, "I want to talk this morning regarding the relationship of the East and West with special consideration for the psychological and theological implications for Christian Mission."

Many of these words the old man had never heard. He paused for a moment and then turned to the congregation and said, "Mama is glad she is here."

From a conference address

Complaints

After examining the contents of the employee's "suggestion box" he had put up, the boss complained, "I wish they would be more specific. What kind of kite? What lake?"

Congress

The late congressman Claude Pepper used to tell the story of the congressman and the bishop who arrived in heaven together and how the congressman was given a lavish suite of rooms, while the bishop was assigned a small, barren room with no view. When the bishop commented on this, St. Peter said he knew how he felt, but explained, "We have thousands of bishops up here; but this is the first congressman we ever got."

Creation

A teacher reports that she had her class write an account of creation. One little girl wrote this:

"God first created Adam. He looked at him and said, 'I think I can do better if I tried again.' So he created Eve."

Lynn H. Rupert

Crowded Pews

One time Tennessee Ernie Ford visited his home church in Tennessee. Many of his relatives were with him in the center section toward the front. News of his attendance brought a packed church with standing room only. The Methodist pastor said nothing about the presence of the famous guest until time for the offering. Then he looked down and thanked Ernie for being there that morning, and added, "Bless your little pew-packing heart!"

Told to me by a member of that church

D

Danger

There is an old story about a Portuguese monastery which was perched high on a 300-foot cliff. Visitors to the monastery were strapped into a big basket, big enough for three persons. Then, they were pulled up to the top of the cliff with a frayed old rope. One passenger, half-way up, inquired nervously, "How often do you change the rope?"

"Whenever the old rope breaks," was the reply from the monk in charge.

Clarence Forsberg

Death

It's an old but usable one which tells of the old man who is dying and the preacher asks, "Have you made peace with God by renouncing the devil and all his works?"

The man answers, "I have made peace with God but I am in no position to antagonize anybody."

Lynn H. Rupert

The missionary saw the Chinese strewing rice over the graves of his ancestors and said to him, "When do you expect your departed ones to come back and eat the rice?"

The Chinese man replied, "At about the same time your ancestors come back and smell the flowers."

Heard in the 1950s

A man picked up the morning paper and read his obituary in the section on death notices. He went down to the newspaper

34

office asking to see who had written it. He was shown a cub reporter to whom he said, "I am not dead. You can see I am very much alive. Now I demand you write a retraction for tomorrow's paper."

The reporter replied, "I never retract a story. But I tell you what I will do: I'll put you in the birth column and give you a fresh start."

H.R.

Definitions

Dennis Erickson, the University of Miami football coach, gives his definition of a fan: "A guy who sits on the 40-yard line, criticizes the coaches and the players, and has all the answers. Then he leaves the stadium and can't find his car."

Sports Illustrated

A boy in school when asked to define the word "widow," said, "A widow is a woman that lived so long with her husband that he died."

"The poor have kinfolks, the well-to-do have relatives, but the wealthy have heirs."

Diplomacy is the art of saying "nice doggie" while you're looking around for a rock.

Three fellows were arguing about how you define the word fame. One said, "Fame is being invited to the White House for a talk with the President in the oval office."

The second fellow claimed that "Fame is being invited to the White House for a talk with the President — when the Hot Line rings and interrupts the conversation, he doesn't answer it."

But the third one topped them both: "You're both wrong. Fame is being invited to the White House for a talk with the President and when the Hot Line rings, he does answer it. He listens a moment, then hands you the phone and says, 'Here, it's for you.' "

My father used to define a *traffic light* as a green light that turns red as you approach.

An *optimist* is a person who sets aside two hours to do his income tax return.

A *pessimist* is a person who expects nothing on a silver tray except tarnish.

An *optimist* is the lady in church who, when she hears the preacher say "In conclusion" begins to put on her shoes. But, the more optimistic person is the deaf man across the aisle from her, who when he sees her begin to put on her shoes, turns on his hearing aid!

H.R.

A Chicago school boy wrote on a science paper, "*Steam* is water that has gone crazy with heat."

An *optimist* can be defined as a fisherman who takes along a camera.

A *hypochondriac* isn't just a person who is forever taking his own temperature; it's one who refuses to believe the thermometer when it registers "normal."

Courage is leaving a restaurant where you have just dined without leaving a healthy tip. *Temerity* is going back to the same restaurant for lunch the next day.

A *consultant* has been defined as a person who charges for telling you what time it is after borrowing your watch.

36

Three years in Boston enabled me to understand the midwesterner who defined "parochial" or "provincial" simply as "Boston." The standing joke then was about the woman who had made an automobile trip to California. On return, someone asked her what route she took. She said she went by way of Dedham (a Boston suburb). Another concerned the lady who said she had a great-niece who was in college "out west." On inquiry, she said the girl was at Vassar which is in Poughkeepsie, New York.

Of course, I have to confess that on a recent trip to San Francisco, I met a man who said he had taken a trip to the east once. "Where to?" I asked. "To Denver," he said. Well, Denver is *east* of California and Poughkeepsie is *west* of Boston!

H.R.

Devil

Two youngsters were walking home from Sunday school where they had heard a lesson on the devil.

"What do you think about all that devil stuff?" one asked.

"Well," replied the other thoughtfully, "you know how Santa Claus turned out. It's probably just your dad."

Diet

One of my father's oldest stories told of the boy at the table for Thanksgiving dinner with his family. He had eaten far more than his share of the goodies on the table. But, he asked for a third helping of turkey. His mother responded, "Why, Tommy, if you eat another bite of turkey, you will burst."

"Okay, Mother," he said, "Just pass the turkey and get out of the way."

Lynn H. Rupert

Diplomacy

One of the late Bishop Kenneth Shanblin's stories was about a man who worked in a supermarket. One day a woman came to the produce department and said she wanted a half-a-grapefruit. The man said they didn't sell half-a-grapefruit. She insisted that was what she wanted. He repeated what he had said. When she kept insisting, he walked into the manager's office, not knowing that she had followed him. He looked at the manager and said, "There's a crazy lady out here who wants to buy half-a-grapefruit." And then he realized that she was standing right beside him, so he added, "And this lovely lady wants to buy the other half." She left and went back to produce while he stood there talking to the manager who said, "That's the fastest recovery I've ever seen in my life. I have never seen quicker mental gymnastics. Where are you from?" The clerk replied, "Baltimore — the hometown of ugly women and a great football team." The manager then said, "That's interesting; my wife's from Baltimore." And the man said, "What position does she play?"

Barry Bailey

Do-It-Yourself

Barry Bailey reports that in his hometown of Sheridan, Arkansas, there is a filling station which maintains a full-time mechanic. There is a sign that lists its rates. It costs $14.50 per hour to have them work on your car. If you watch, it costs $16.50; if you help, it costs $18.50. And, if you worked on it before you brought it in to them, it costs $21.50.

Barry Bailey

Have you ever tried to put together a two-story pasteboard dollhouse on Christmas Eve? I had kept putting it off with the excuse that our two girls might see it before they should. So, I was working away into the wee hours as Christmas dawned. Nothing seemed to work out just right. It looked easy.

Then, when I was looking down in the carton it came in for what I thought was a missing piece, I found a small white card with these words printed on it, "If all else fails, follow the directions."

H.R.

Dogs

There was the youngster who claimed to have the smartest dog ever. "All I have to say to the dog," the boy explained, "is 'are you coming or aren't you?' And he either comes or he doesn't."

A little boy looked with longing at his friend's dog, and said, "I want a dog for Christmas, but my folks say I can't have one."

"You didn't ask right," his friend advised. "Ask for a baby brother. Then you'll get the dog."

The Baptist Record

The old hunter had just bought a new retriever. He took the dog out for a trial. When a flock of geese went over, he shot one and it fell in the water. He told the dog, "Go get him, Wilbur." And Wilbur took off right over the top of the water, grabbed the goose and brought it back. Later the amazed hunter decided to show off his water-walking dog. He invited a friend to go hunting the next day. Another flock of geese flew over and the hunter brought one down. Again Wilbur trotted across the water and retrieved it. "Did you notice anything unusual about my dog?" the hunter asked proudly. "Yeah," replied his friend, "he can't swim."

American Opinion

Doctors

A man who was fed up with the world and its grim promise of war and conflict was being examined for new glasses. He said to the doctor, "I would like to see things a little less clearly, please."

Drinking

Another story that has several versions is the one about the modern miracle of transforming water into wine. My version has it that an American was trying to smuggle some tequila from Mexico into the U.S. He had it in a large thermos. The customs man asked what was in it. He replied, "Just cold water for our journey." The suspicious customs man opened it, smelled it, and then tasted it. "Sir, this is tequila," he said. And the man replied, "The Lord's done it again — a modern miracle!"

E

Ecumenical

How church folk react to fire:

There was once an ecumenical gathering being held in a building when someone came in and shouted, "The building is on fire!"

The Methodists gathered in a corner and prayed.

The Baptists cried, "Where's the water?"

The Christian Scientists agreed among themselves that there was no fire.

The Fundamentalists shouted, "It is the vengeance of the Lord."

The Lutherans posted a notice on the door declaring the fire was evil.

The Quakers quietly praised God for the blessing which fire brings.

The Jews posted symbols on the doors, hoping the fire would pass.

The Episcopalians formed a procession and marched out in grand style.

The Congregationalists and the Southern Baptists shouted, "Every man for himself!"

And the Presbyterians appointed a chairman, who was to appoint a committee to look into the whole matter.

Seen in church bulletins, author unknown

Epitaphs

"Here lies Lester Moor,
Four slugs from a 44,
No less, no more." *(The old west)*

A dentist:
"Stranger! Approach this spot with gravity
John Brown is filling his last cavity."

An editor:
"Here lies an editor! Snooks if you will;
In mercy, King Providence, let him lie still!
He lied for a living; so he lived while he lied;
When he could not lie longer, he lied down and died."

A bookseller:
"Here lies poor Ned Pardon, from misery freed,
Who long was a bookseller's hack;
He led such a miserable life in this world,
I don't think he'll ever come back."

A haberdasher:
"Here lies John Smith,
Sometimes hosier and haberdasher in this town.
He left his house, his Anna, his love,
To sing hosanna in the realms above."

Connecticut:
"Here lies, cut down like unripe fruit,
The wife of Deacon Amos Shute:
She died drinking too much coffee,
Anny dominy eighteen forty." (But what was her name?)

New Jersey:
"She was not smart, she was not fair,
But hearts with grief for her are swellin';
And empty stands her little chair;
She died of eatin' watermelon."

from C. Thomas Hilton, The Clergy Journal

Ft. Wallace, Kansas:
"He tried to make 2 jacks beat a pair of aces."

Middletown, Maryland:
"I fought a good battle, but I losted."

Elkhart, Indiana, professor:
"School is out
Teacher has gone home."

Ruido, New Mexico:
"Here lies John Yeast;
Pardon me for not rising."

Lee County, Mississippi:
"Once I wasn't
Then I was
Now I ain't
Again" — *Clergy talk*

Hypochondriac:
"I told you I was sick."

Holly, Michigan, cemetery:
"He did not reach 70 going like 60."

More epitaphs from various unknown sources which I have collected:

Wall Street Trinity Church:
"Remember friends as you pass by,
As you are now, so once was I.
So, as I am you soon will be,
So prepare for death and follow me."

Maryland:
"Here lies the body of Jane Smith, wife of Thomas Smith, a marble cutter. This monument, erected as a tribute to her memory, may be duplicated for $250."

Exams

Dr. Robert Palmer tells of a student who failed to prepare adequately for his final examination. He took it anyway and failed miserably. Hoping the professor might be lenient, he wrote on the last page of the blue book: "Blessed are the merciful —."

Even with leniency, the prof had to mark the exam "F." But after the letter grade, wrote, "Blessed are those who mourn —."

Donald J. Shelby

On another exam a student wrote, "Only God knows the answers to these questions, I know I don't." The professor wrote back: "God gets an A and you get an F."

Excuses

One Sunday Barry Bailey's televised service lost its sound for about a minute. When he learned of this later, he started checking into where the trouble was. They found someone had made a mistake. In discussing this with him, this person was serious when he explained, "But you must realize that we do a good job most of the time." Then Bailey imagines an airplane pilot who flies for five hours saying, "I only crashed for 20 seconds" or a doctor who says, "The operation was going nicely except for the 25 seconds when the patient died."

Barry Bailey

Casey Stengel said he could never stand to have a "pebble-picker" in his infield lineup. A pebble-picker is the short-stop who, when he misses a grounder, looks around on the infield and always finds a pebble and holds it up as an excuse for his error.

Heard at a sports banquet, 1965

Exercise

Someone has said the only exercise that some people take is dodging the issues, sidestepping responsibilities, climbing walls of irritability, running down their friends, and passing the buck.

Expectations

Some things never turn out to be as big as you expected:

The "two acres of woodland" surrounding a picturesque cabin.

The lakeside cabin which is a mile from any body of water.

The half-gallon of ice cream you bring home for the children's party.

The "generous sample" you're sent free on request.

The "surprise gift" you are to receive for your first mail order.

Your salary raise after it has formed a merger with your deductions.

The gas mileage on your new car.

The proof of your recent photographic efforts.

The church to which you have been assigned as pastor.

Coverages on your car insurance.

Collected from various sources

F

Faith

During World War II, in a Humphrey Bogart movie, a sailor says he has faith in God, FDR, and the Brooklyn Dodgers — in that order. So, he says, the war will be won.

Sir Cedrick Hardwick, the British actor, was on a trans-Atlantic flight in the pre-jet days. The plane developed engine trouble and made an emergency landing in Gander, Newfoundland. As the plane rolled to a stop, Hardwick, feeling very relieved himself, turned to the proverbial little old lady next to him and asked if she had been frightened.

"Heavens no," she said. "Why it wasn't even on our side of the plane."

Ray E. Balcomb

Leslie Weatherhead told of a group during the London blitzkrieg in World War II who were discussing faith and courage and the ability to sleep at night with the bombs bursting in air, and sometimes very close. One woman, a domestic cleaning woman said, "Our preacher says that God neither slumbers nor sleeps. And so I argues — What's the good of both God and me lying awake? So, I just says my prayers and then I says, 'To hell with Hitler,' and then I goes to sleep!"

Family

The new neighbor was talking with a seven-year-old boy living next door. She wanted to know how many kids there were in his family. He told her there were eight.

She said, "My goodness, that many children must cost a lot of money."

"Oh, we don't buy them. We raise them," replied the boy.

Lynn H. Rupert

Father

The teacher asked the new arrival in kindergarten what her father's name was.

"Daddy," replied the little girl.

"No, I mean his first name — what does your mother call him?"

"She doesn't call him anything," explained the little one. "She likes him."

Two youngsters were discussing their fathers, especially the little peculiarities of their behavior. One asked the other, "Does your daddy have a den?"

"Nope," said his little friend. "He just growls all over the place at our house."

Farm And Farmers

The proverbial city child was getting his first glimpse of farm life. He sat down beside the farmer's wife who was in the process of plucking a chicken. The youngster watched her for a while and then asked, "Do you take off their clothes every night?"

Williams

Fire

An oil well caught fire in Oklahoma. The owners called in professional help, but their efforts were in vain. A second

47

group of pros was working on the well when the fire truck from the nearby town came racing over a nearby hill, manned by its volunteer department members. It came racing down the hill toward the fiery rig, and, with people scattering to get out of the way, the truck drove squarely over the well and, in so doing, miraculously put out the fire. The owners came up to the volunteer chief who had been driving the truck, and said to him, "This is fantastic. You have saved us thousands of dollars. As a token of our gratitude we want to give your fire department a check for $100,000."

Reporters crowded around and asked the chief what they would be doing with this windfall. The chief responded, "Well, the first thing I am going to do is get the brakes fixed on this truck."

Heard at annual conference, 1972

Fishing

Mark Twain once said, "Do not tell fish stories where the people know you; but particularly don't tell them where they know the fish."

The mother suggested to Junior that he take his little sister with him fishing that day.

"No ma'am," said Junior firmly, "the last time she tagged along I didn't catch one fish."

"I'm sure she will be quiet this time," said his mother.

"It wasn't the noise," Junior explained. "She ate the bait."

A little girl came running back from the river and yelled to her father that a man had chased her.

"What did you do?" asked her father.

"Nothing," she replied breathlessly, "except he was fishing and had some big fish laying in the sand and they were going to die, so I put them back in the water."

48

Flattery

An office boy noticed two women at lunch with his boss. Later in the day he asked who those women were. The boss replied that one was his wife and the other was Elizabeth Taylor.

"Which one was Elizabeth Taylor?" asked the boy.

The boss took out a $5 bill and handed it to the lad who wanted to know what this was for.

"Nothing," replied the boss. "I just wanted you to remember when you get to be president, that I once loaned you money."

Clergy Talk

Flood

A man who had survived the Johnstown Flood, and ever since plagued any listener with the full account of his experience, finally reached the age where he wished to die and go to heaven where he could tell the story. Picture his consternation when he did indeed get his wish, and had gathered an audience to tell them about the flood, only to discover Noah sitting in the front row.

Fool And Fooled

Henry Ward Beecher was a controversial preacher and received letters that were condemnatory. One Sunday he took one of these letters into his Plymouth Church pulpit, and showed it to his congregation. It contained one word, "Fool." Beecher said that he had received many letters from persons who had forgotten to sign their names, but this was the first time he had known of a man signing his name and forgetting to write the letter.

Football

One university football coach has announced he is going to try the three-squad system this year. One will play offense. One will play defense. And the third squad will attend class.

Notre Dame football coach, Lou Holtz, talking about job security said, "I have a lifetime contract. That means I cannot be fired during the third quarter if we are ahead and moving the ball."

Forgiveness

Two sisters kept up a feud in Scotland for 30 years. Alice visited Mary when she was sick in the hospital. Mary looked at her sternly and said, "The doctors say I'm seriously ill, Alice. If I die, I want you to know you are forgiven. But, if I pull through, things stay as they are."

In Mark Twain's autobiography, he wrote a scathing denunciation against a publisher who had swindled him out of a lot of money. But he made it seem he was ending on a note of forgiveness when he wrote, "He has been dead now for a quarter of a century. I have only compassion for him, and if I could, I would send him a fan."

Most of us would not be as forgiving as a man in Oklahoma City who was late for an appointment downtown. He was completely frustrated when, after searching in vain for a parking place, he saw that a car had parked in such a way that it occupied two places right in front of the building where he was going. His sense of humor conquered his frustration and he double parked, wrote a note, and put it under the windshield wiper of the illegally parked car. The note said: "Congratulations. You have found two parking places while I have spent 15 minutes in looking and haven't found one!"

News item

Funerals

A Texas preacher was asked to conduct the funeral for a known gangster. Others of his mob waited on the pastor and demanded that he make it a service of praise for the departed brother who had been sent home to glory by a rival mob. They told the pastor what terrible things might happen to him if he didn't do what they asked.

Meanwhile, his board of deacons met and agreed that any person has the right to a burial service, but they warned him not to pray the brother into heaven.

Caught on the horns of this dilemma, the preacher began the service: "Brothers and sisters, I propose to funeralize our departed brother to the River Jordan and let whosoever's he is come and get him there."

I heard former Ohio Governor Lausche tell this

A farmer tells the story of the funeral of Punk Green's mother-in-law, who was kicked to death by his mule. The church was overflowing with people at her funeral. One of her friends crowded in and said, "Punk, your mother-in-law must have been mighty popular around these parts to get such a turnout for her funeral."

Punk replied, "Well, actually they didn't really come for the funeral. They came to buy the old mule."

The old man was near death. His children crowded around the bed to hear his last words. Finally, he said, "Kids, your

51

mother and I have been married for more than 50 years, and she's the best cook I've ever known. Even now, at death's door I can smell a strudel baking. Sarah, daughter, be good and go get me a piece of it before I die."

Sarah went and after a minute returned without the requested delicacy.

"Where is the strudel I asked for?" her father asked.

"Mama says you can't have any. It's for the funeral reception."

Following the funeral they had gathered to hear the reading of the will of their wealthy relative and employer. The attorney read: "To my cousin, Osgood, I leave my stock portfolio and properties on the Outer Cape ... to my faithful cook, Minnie, I leave my Palm Beach estate ... to George, my chauffeur and handyman who served me so well, I leave $100,000 in cash ... and to my nephew Brutus, who always argued that health is more important than wealth, I leave my sweat socks and jogging shoes."

A funeral procession, with the funeral coach and limousines, was moving along. Directly behind the funeral coach was a Brink's truck. Two men were standing on the street observing the procession and one says to the other, "Well, old George did say he was going to take it with him one way or another."

H.R.

My friend Dr. Donald Miller, Presbyterian clergyman, told me of a graveside service he once conducted which was for a man from military service. The gun salute followed. The deceased man's mother was sitting in a chair in front of the casket. When the first gun blast went off, it scared her so she fell off the chair. Her little grandson, standing nearby screamed, "They shot Grandma!"

Donald Miller

52

There was the rich man in Virginia who had asked to be buried at the wheel of his Cadillac. Two men watched as they drove the car into the grave over the ramp which had been dug down to it. The corpse was sitting all dressed up at the wheel. One man commented, "Boy, that's really livin'!"

H.R.

A funeral director found that his hearse had developed a bad squeak which was not well-received by those in the funeral procession. His staff couldn't find it. So he took it to his mechanic. He couldn't be sure what to do until he had heard the squeak. So, the funeral director drove him down the street. The mechanic lay down on the back floor of the hearse and listened for the noise. At the first stop light he sat up and looked around. Two women fainted and the cars in the lane next to his slammed into each other as their drivers went into shock.

H.R.

Speaking of funerals and burials, there is now available, for those who feel they will not have enough time while alive to say their say, a "talking tombstone." For $10,000 you can purchase this monument with a built-in speaker that features a 90-minute recorded message which you can make, while alive, to be played back after your death and burial. The playback mechanism for this modern version of Enochism is powered by solar energy and activated by a key — so in a sense is eternal! (As the Bible says, "He being dead, yet speaketh.")

News item

G

God

A little boy one day wrote a letter to God. In it he said, "Dear Mr. God: How do you feel about people who don't believe in you?" He signed his name and then added a post script, "Somebody else wants to know."

Clarence Forsberg

An old farmer and his wife were "sitting out" an electrical storm. He chewed away on his tobacco and occasionally lifted the stove lid to spit into the fire. His wife sat there wringing her hands, very much afraid.

After lightning had struck a nearby tree, she wailed, "Pa, the Lord's goin' to destroy the world."

"Wal," said Pa, "it's his'n, ain't it?"

Quote

A cub reporter was sent out from New York to cover the Johnstown flood. He wired back his first story with this lead line, "God sits on the hillside above Johnstown tonight, and weeps —"

A reply wire soon arrived from his editor which said, "Forget the flood, get an interview with God."

Heard in the 1960s

It was in the days of the open Pullman car on trains. The little girl was in an upper berth while her parents occupied the berth just beneath her. She was afraid and kept asking her mother if she was there, and then her father if he was there. This went on for some time, keeping the whole sleeping car personnel awake.

Finally, one man in a berth across the aisle called out, "Little girl, your mother is here, your father is here, I am here, we are all here. Will you please be quiet and go to sleep!"

After a moment, in a weak voice the child asked, "Mama, was that God?"

H.R.

In Sunday school the little girl said God was in their bathroom at home. When pressed for details, she explained simply, "Every morning, my father comes out in the hall and bangs on the bathroom door and says, 'God, are you still in there?' "

My sister, Mary Masterson (at age 7)

Grandparents

Someone has observed, "Grandchildren are those remarkable individuals who have managed to inherit all of your good qualities, and none of their parents' faults."

Guilt

Sir Arthur Conan Doyle, detective story author, once sent a telegram to each of 12 friends, all men of great virtue and considerable position in British society. The message: "Fly At Once; All Is Discovered."

Within 24 hours all 12 had left the country.

American Opinion

H

Half-Truths

In his autobiography, the late Senator Claude Pepper recalled that in his last senatorial campaign, which he lost, his opponent was not above character assassination. He circulated, among the "rednecks" in the boondocks of Florida, the following statement about Mr. Pepper: "Are you aware that Claude Pepper is known all over as a shameless extrovert? Not only that but this man is reliably reported to practice nepotism with his sister-in-law, and he has a sister who once was a thespian in wicked New York. Worst of all, it is an established fact that Mr. Pepper, before his marriage, habitually practiced celibacy."

Happiness

Will Rogers used to talk about a druggist who was asked if he ever took time off to have a good time. The druggist said, "No, but I sold a lot of headache medicine to those who did."

J. Wallace Hamilton

Hearing

An Episcopal congregation in Florida installed a sound system on a trial basis. One reaction: "If I had wanted to hear, I would have moved up front."

Context

Heaven

St. Peter was talking to some new arrivals in heaven. They were asking a lot of questions about heaven. They asked about one group.

"These people," said Peter, "are dancing and partying because on earth their religion did not let them have any fun dancing and partying."

"Who are those over there?" they asked, pointing in another direction.

"Those people are playing golf and watching sporting events because on earth their religion would not let them do anything like that."

Then they asked, "Who are those people over there reading and watching movies?"

"They were not allowed to do that on earth because of their religion."

"Well then," said the new arrivals, "who are those people over there just sitting around doing nothing and looking bored?"

"Well," said Peter, "those are my Presbyterians. They were able to do everything on earth and so now there is little left for them to do and enjoy here in heaven."

C. Thomas Hilton, The Clergy Journal

The pastor was calling on the residents of a country home. He was sitting in the parlor with his hostess when her small son and his friend came dashing in carrying a dead rat. Excitedly, the boy said to his mother, "Don't worry, Mother, he's dead. We hit him and bashed him and stomped him until —" then he noticed the minister for the first time, and added in a lowered voice, "until God called him home."

H.R.

Health

A preacher was in the hospital. A nurse's aide was making the rounds of rooms to take temperatures. He was half asleep when she shoved the tube in his mouth and went on her way. She came back and then recorded the temperature on the chart at the foot of his bed. Soon after this the doctor came in and picked up the chart. As he read it, he almost exploded, thus alarming the preacher. The doctor called the aide and asked what she had done to the patient. She said she took his temperature. "What did you use?" And she showed him. He snorted, "Miss, this is a barometer!" Then he asked the preacher if he wanted to know what his temperature report said. He did, and the doctor read from the chart, "Dry and windy!"

H.R.

Hell

And of course you remember the fellow who arrived in Hell and started ordering everyone around. Someone said to him, "You act like you own this place."

"I do," he said, "My wife gave it to me just before I left."

H.R.

A bus overturned, killing all the members of UMW Circle. When they arrived at the Pearly Gates, St. Peter greeted them with the "No Vacancy" sign. He was embarrassed since they all deserved to be in heaven. But they were building a new sub-division in heaven and they would have to reside temporarily in Hell.

They had been in Hell for about three weeks when Satan called St. Peter, frantically begging him to take the circle ladies back. But St. Peter allowed as to still having his housing problems.

"Problems?" You don't know what problems are!" Satan roared. "With their bake sales, rummage sales and bazaars, these women need only $40 more to air condition this place!"

H.R. (one of several versions)

58

Husbands And Wives

A woman was fed up with the boring conferences she had to have with her lawyer in her divorce proceedings and was complaining to a friend.

The friend responded, "Oh, don't talk to me about your complaints. I've had so much trouble over my property that sometimes I wish my husband hadn't died."

Frank Dickson in Quote, June 4, 1967

A wife was telling her husband at breakfast of a curious dream she had had the night before. "I dreamt I was dead," she said, "and was on my way to heaven. At the foot of Jacob's ladder I was handed a piece of chalk with instructions to put a cross on each step for each sin I committed. When I was only a short way up, I met you coming down."

"Refused admittance?" he asked.

"No, dear, you were going to get more chalk."

Cappers

I-J

Impossible

A self-service elevator had a sign which said, "Eighth Floor Button Out of Order. Please push Five and Three."

Inheritance

The professor had just finished a lecture on evolution. He asked for class discussion. One fellow raised his hand and said, "I'm already the sort of person I'll be, so I can't see what difference it would make to me if my great-grandfather had been an ape."

"You're right," said the professor, "but just think what a difference it would have made to your great-grandfather!"

Joan Welsh in Quote

Jesus

The late Harold Bosley said his six-year-old granddaughter returned from Sunday school one Sunday, singing with great gusto, "Jesus Loves Me." Her father asked, "Do you really think Jesus loves you?" She stopped her singing and said, "He doesn't even know me!"

K

Kids

A minister asked a group of children in Sunday school, "Why do you love God?" The best response was, "I don't know. I guess it just runs in the family."

A little girl was saying her prayers one evening at her bedside. Her aunt was visiting and heard the prayer. She commented to the little girl: "It's a pleasure to hear you saying your prayers so well. You speak so earnestly and seriously, and you seem to really mean what you say, and care about it too."

"Well, auntie," the little girl said, "you should hear me gargle!"

On my 30th birthday, the children's department leaders asked me to come there during Sunday school because the children wanted to sing their birthday song for me. When I got there, they sang, and then one child presented me an empty dish which he explained was for my birthday offering — one penny for each year. I did have a quarter and a nickel but no pennies. The teacher suggested I change the 30 cents in the regular offering dish — which I did, finding enough pennies there. She explained that the children liked to count as the pennies were put in one by one. And they did, and we had a good time because "Dr. Rupert is so old."

That afternoon we had a meeting at the church at which several sets of parents were in attendance. They all seemed to have gotten the message that "Dr. Rupert took 30 pennies out of our offering to put in his birthday offering!"

H.R.

The youngster had been naughty. Her father had given her a hard time over it both by word and punishment. That night when he turned down the covers on his bed, he found a note on his pillow which said, in childish scrawl, "Be kind to your children and they will be kind to you." Signed GOD.

H.R.

The youngster wanted to use the Bible name "Lo" when the class was saying which Bible name they would like to have. He too, was a close friend of Jesus who said, "Lo, I will be with you always."

L

Language

Two American sailors were on leave while their ship was docked in Stockholm. They were church-going Methodists, so Sunday morning they looked up the nearest Methodist Church. The people, of course, spoke Swedish, the bulletin and hymnal were in Swedish. They agreed that they would watch the young man who sat in the same pew with them. They would stand when he did, kneel when he did, etc. This worked well, until the pastor came down from the chancel and spoke informally. With a big smile he said something and pointed in the direction of their pew. They watched as the young man stood up, so they stood up too. The whole congregation and the pastor burst out laughing.

Later someone who spoke English explained the laughter to the young Americans.

"The pastor announced that a new baby had been born to a parish family just the night before and he asked the new father to stand — and you stood up along with him!"

Heard in Stockholm, H.R.

Law

In Chicago it is against the law to eat in a place that is on fire.

In Oklahoma there is a law which prohibits catching a whale in the inland waters of that state.

A homiletical law: In those places in your sermon where the argument is vague or weak, yell like hell.

Lazy

A coffee break can be characterized as follows:

a. A 10-minute suspension of work that always lasts a half hour.

b. A period of conversation not limited to fact or knowledge.

c. The primary method of office communication.

d. Everyone's favorite method of achieving maximum alertness in time for that period generally designated as lunch.

Found on a coffee mug

Lies

Asked by his Sunday school teacher to define a lie, the boy said, "A lie is an abomination to the Lord and a very present help in trouble."

C. Rex Bevins

M

Marriage

A woman bought 200 stamps in the Lynnfield, Massachusetts, post office. They were for her daughter's wedding invitations. An hour later she returned to exchange them explaining that her daughter thought the whooping crane on the stamps looked too much like a stork.

Grit

Medicine And Medical

Medical terminology for the layperson:
Artery — the study of fine paintings
Barium — what you do when CPR fails
Caesarean Section — a district in the city of Rome
Colic — a sheep dog
Coma — a punctuation mark
Congenital — friendly
Dilate — to live a long time
Fester — quicker
G.I. Series — baseball games between teams of soldiers
Grippe — a suitcase
Hangnail — a coat hook
Medical staff — a doctor's cane
Minor operation — digging for coal
Morbid — a higher offer
Nitrate — lower than the day rate
Node — was aware of
Organic — musical
Outpatient — a person who has fainted

Post-operative — a letter carrier
Protein — in favor of young people
Secretion — hiding anything
Tablet — a small table
Tumor — an extra pair
Varicose veins — veins which are very close together

Author unknown (I think I know why)

Methodists

A bandit confronted a Methodist circuit rider in an isolated area as the parson was riding to his next preaching place. The bandit made him get off his horse and started to rummage through his saddlebags. The preacher said, "You wouldn't rob a poor Methodist preacher, would you, sir?" "I am sorry," said the highwayman, "I didn't realize you were a preacher, what brand are you?" "I'm a Methodist," was the reply. "Of course I won't rob you. I am a Methodist myself."

H.R.

Money

A woman inquired of a Methodist minister if he would baptize her dog. He replied, with as much dignity as he could muster, that baptism was for people not animals.

The woman went on, "I would be glad to give you $100 for baptizing my dog."

"Madam," he inquired, "Was your dog born a Methodist?"

Raymond F. Balcomb

Vance Packard reported that he saw on a Chicago billboard this message; "Now you can borrow enough to get completely out of debt."

66

A man needed $100 right away. In desperation he wrote a letter to God explaining his situation. It arrived at the Dead Letter office since it was addressed only to "God." The employee who opened it was so moved by the man's need that he passed the hat among his PO colleagues. They raised $75 and put it in an envelope mailed to this man, care of General Delivery. The man got the letter, opened it, counted the money, and then scribbled off another letter addressed to God. When the PO employees opened the second letter, it said: "Dear God, the money arrived $25 short. Please make up the difference, but don't send it through the Post Office because it is full of thieves."

Clarence Forsberg

Music

Jack Benny told of the time he carried his violin case to the White House to play for the President. A guard stopped him and asked what was in the case.

To be funny, Benny replied, "A machine gun."

"Thank goodness," dead panned the guard, "I was afraid it was your violin."

N

Names

Then, of course, there was a coal miner in West Virginia whose wife had twins. He named then Anthracite and Bituminous.

Once in a youth group in a rural Kansas church we had three sisters named Queen Bee, Honey Bee and Sunshine.

H.R.

Nepotism

Some years ago Russ Hedderly, then a linebacker for Kent State, was named to some pre-season All-American teams. He said, "I don't know about any place else in the conference, but I know I'll always be called the leading tackler at our home games. My dad is the public address announcer."

Nervous

It's an old one and variously told. But, a woman entered a room in a Washington, D.C. hotel and found there was a man whom she recognized as a well-known government official. He was pacing up and down and she asked him what he was doing there. "I am going to deliver a speech," he said.

"Do you usually get very nervous before addressing a large audience?"

"Nervous?" he replied. "No, I never get nervous."

"In that case," demanded the lady, "what are you doing in the Ladies Room?"

News story

Offering

A certain church was taking a missionary offering. As the plate was passed to one dour-faced man, he growled, "I don't believe in missions."

The usher replied, "Well, then take some out, brother, this offering is for the heathen."

Lynn H. Rupert

They were taking the annual pre-Christmas offering for the poor and needy. The pastor took one look at the offering plate as it was returning to the altar, then he looked over the people and inquired, "Will the real Ebenezer Scrooge please stand up?"

Charles Cartwright had a cartoon which showed the minister about to receive the offering. He said, "And now, brothers and sisters, let us all give in accordance with what we reported on Form 1040, IRS."

I heard this well-travelled story about the Roman Catholic Bishop of Akron, Ohio. He was seated next to an IRS official at a banquet. The man said to the bishop, "It must bring you a lot of joy and satisfaction to receive such large contributions as Mr _____ gives your diocese." He named a high official in one of the rubber companies.

The bishop looked a bit startled, and asked who did he say it was.

The IRS man again named the man, and said, "He did give you diocese $10,000 last year, didn't he?"

"No," said the bishop, "but he will, he will!"

The pastor walked into the vestry and was shocked to find his wife with both hands in the collection plate.

"Ethel," he shouted, "what in the world do you think you're doing?"

His wife replied, "I'm looking for a button to sew on your coat."

A story out of my boyhood as a PK: four boys were bragging about their father's income. The doctor's son said that his father would work a few minutes in the operating room and receive a thousand dollars. The investment banker's son said that his father could take a few minutes in making some stock purchases and he would get $2,000 profit within the hour. The lawyer's son said his father could go to court for a few days and come out with $10,000. But the preacher's kid said that every Sunday his father stood up and made a little speech and then took an offering and it took eight men to carry it out."

Church sign: "The Lord loveth a cheerful giver, but he also accepteth from a mean old grouch."

Before the offering, the minister announced, "I have noticed a man in the congregation who has been flirting with a member of the choir throughout the service. Unless I find a $5 bill in the offering plate, I will be tempted to tell his wife." When they counted the offering in the little church, there were seven $5 bills.

One-Liners

Yogi Berra: "If people don't want to come to the ball game, there's no way you can stop them."

"You are only young once, but you can remain immature all your life."

From Jerry Glanville, former coach of the NFL Houston Oilers:

"When I was born, the doctor looked at me and spanked my mom."

On a 300-pound player he cut from the squad, "This guy was so fat it looked like someone sat in his lap and didn't leave."

On why he would never own a horse, "I don't want to keep anything that eats while I'm sleeping, including a wife."

When Glanville got to Houston in 1984, he says, "We had the nicest guys in the NFL. Their mamas loved 'em. Their daddies loved 'em. But they wouldn't hit if you handed 'em sticks."

Sports Illustrated

"There's no place like home, which is why motels are so popular."

"Every man has his price and mine is extremely low."

"A penny saved is hardly worth the effort."

"Beauty is skin deep, which is adequate as far as I'm concerned."

"Let sleeping dogs lie, they seldom tell the truth anyway."

"Where there's a will, there's a wave of nieces and nephews."

"You can't take it with you, but you can sure have fun with it while you're here."

"He who laughs last won't be with the company for long."

P

Parachutes

The small plane was carrying three passengers — a Boy Scout, a bishop and a brilliant statesman. The pilot warned of an impending crash. Then he said, "Unfortunately, we have only three parachutes. I must take one so I can report the accident to the proper authorities."

"I must have one parachute," said the brilliant statesman, "because I have a great contribution to make for mankind." He jumped after the pilot.

"The bishop turned to the Scout and said, "My son, I've lived a long life. Your life lies ahead of you. You take the last parachute — good luck."

"Don't worry, your grace," said the Scout. "We've got two parachutes. The brilliant statesman took my knapsack."

Heard first at Rotary Club, 1970s

Perfection

The legendary Ted Williams had had a particularly great day even for him. He had hit two homers, was four-for-four at the plate and had knocked in five runs. He had done everything just right.

A cub reporter ran into the locker room and said, "Oh Mr. Williams, you did everything today but walk on water."

Whereupon, Ted Williams said to the locker room boy, "Fill the shower! Today's the day!"

Ernest G. Schmidt, "Choose to Win," Abingdon, 1979, page 97

72

Politics

The candidate had given a stirring but fact-filled speech. He confidently asked the audience if there were any questions. "Yes," came a voice from the rear, "Who else is running?"

H.R.

Statements by politicians:
"Being in politics is like being a football coach. You have to be smart enough to understand the game and dumb enough to think it is important." — Eugene McCarthy
"A conservative is a man who just thinks and sits, mostly sits." — Woodrow Wilson
"Blessed are the young, for they shall inherit the national debt." — Herbert Hoover

Prayer

A cartoon depicted a little fellow on his knees beside his bed saying his prayers. He listed all the things he wanted and the things he wanted God to do. Then, as an after-thought he added, "Oh yeah, in case there is anything I can do for you, just let me know, God."

Donald S. Ewing

The ship was sinking and the captain was passing out the life belts. Suddenly he called out to the passengers, and asked if anyone there knew how to pray. A preacher among the passengers eagerly announced that he did.
"Thank goodness for you," said the captain. "We are short one life belt."

It was commencement time at a small Baptist college in the south. Members of the faculty were squirming through a

73

long-winded, disorganized and boring address at the outdoor commencement exercises. One faculty member reports that a note started to circulate among the suffering faculty. It read; "Pray for rain!"

Tom Matheny

The priest asked the boy if he said his prayers before going to bed. He replied, "No, my mother says them."
"What does she say?" asked the priest.
"Thank God, he's in bed."

H.R.

The little boy's grandma lived with his family. She was always complaining about the house being too cold. The father couldn't keep the furnace hot enough. So the boy took to prayer. "God bless mother and father," he prayed, "and make me a good boy. And please make it hot for grandma."

Lynn H. Rupert

While he was governor of California in the 1960s, Ronald Reagan was speaking to a convention of auto industry executives and pointing out that all was not fine in California. He said that the land was under water, the ocean was under oil, the campuses were under siege. He got so discouraged he called Dial-a-Prayer and they hung up on him!

News report of a speech

Then there was the little boy who was asked if he said his prayers every night. He replied, "No, not every night. Some nights I don't want anything."

Preachers

A pastor was out calling on his flock. He came to one house and knocked. No answer. He knocked a little louder. He heard a faint voice coming from somewhere inside the house saying, "Come in. Come in." He tried the door and it was unlocked, so he stepped into the entry hall. No one was there but again he heard the voice off to his left, "Come in." He proceeded into what was the living room, still nobody, but still the voice, now more distinctly. It sounded from the kitchen, "Come in."

He opened the kitchen door and found himself face to face with a fierce, snarling German shepherd dog. The dog lunged toward the preacher and put his two paws on his shoulders, pinning him against the wall.

At that moment the preacher saw a parrot sitting calmly in a cage over to one side, and then it suddenly dawned on him. So he yelled at the bird: "You stupid parrot. Don't you know any other words than 'Come in?' "

And the parrot squawked, "Sic 'em! Sic 'em!"

Clarence Forsberg

Dr. Willsie Martin was a distinguished California Methodist preacher. He told this story on himself. On a Sunday morning, shortly after he had come to the church to get ready for the worship service, he went around to the narthex of the church. The doors were open and he saw an elderly lady slowly and with much effort trying to negotiate the front steps. She had arrived quite early for the service. Being a gentleman, Dr. Martin went down the steps and helped her climb them.

When they got to the top, she turned to him, obviously not recognizing who he was, thanked him and asked who was preaching that morning.

He said with a note of pride, "Why, Willsie Martin, Ma'am!"

She thought a moment and then said, "Will you help me back down the steps, please?"

Mark Trotter

A minister was sent to a church which had the reputation of being difficult to serve and of shipping preachers out after one year each. This man stayed 10 years. The bishop was so impressed he dropped in to see the Pulpit Committee chair. Said the bishop, "This church used to have a horrible reputation, you never kept a pastor for more than a year at a time. We sent you this man and he stayed 10 years. What happened?"

The chair said, "We never wanted a minister in the first place, and this man is the nearest thing to nothing you ever sent us."

C. Rex Bevins

A layman was visiting his pastor in the hospital and said to him with great enthusiasm, "The board passed a resolution last evening hoping for your speedy recovery. The vote was 41-39."

An oldie

One church member said to another, "I have nothing but praise for our new minister."

The other said, "Yes, I noticed that when the offering plate passed."

A preacher moved into a new parish. He was a Rotarian so he attended the local club. The president welcomed him and observed that in this agricultural county seat in Kansas the pastor's predecessor had been a member of the club. The president hoped the new pastor would become a member. He pointed out that the predecessor had won the county hog-calling contest for five years and he hoped the new preacher could continue bringing such an honor to the club.

The preacher responded with words of appreciation for the welcome. Then he said, "Now about this hog-calling bit, let me say the bishop appointed me to come here and be a shepherd to the sheep. But you know your people better than I do."

H.R.

Bishop Melvin Wheatley recalls that when he was a young preacher he tackled one Sunday morning the difficult theme of pain and evil and suffering in the world. At the door following the service, one of his parishioners, wanting to be supporting but not quite phrasing it right said, "Oh, Reverend Wheatley, I don't think I ever really knew what it meant to suffer until I heard you preach."

Mel Wheatley

One of my ministerial colleagues was an usher at the wedding of another of our colleagues. Beards were not common on campus in those years, but Tony had a full beard. As he came back up the aisle from having seated some guests, four-year-old Heidi asked her mother, "Is that Jesus?"

H.R.

This Methodist preacher had been appointed to a church for 20 years which was about 18 years longer than the congregation wanted. Each year they asked the bishop to move the preacher, but each year he sent him back. Finally, after the 20th year and the 18th urgent request from the church, the bishop moved in. The congregation had a reception and invited the minister to say a few words. He said a few words and then concluded with these words, "Jesus called me to this church 20 years ago, and now he is calling me to another field in which to labor."

When he sat down the choir stood and sang, "What a Friend We Have In Jesus."

Mark Trotter

Another old one tells of the Methodist, Presbyterian and Catholic clergy who were together in a boat fishing about 25 yards from shore.

"I am out of bait," said the Methodist, and stepped out of the boat and walked across the water to land.

"I am out of drinking water," said the Presbyterian a little later, and he got out and walked to the shore for water, and then returned.

Finally, without saying anything, the Catholic priest got out of the boat and immediately sank. He came up, got back in the boat, then stepped out again, and sank again.

The Methodist said to the Presbyterian, "Do you think it's time to tell him where the rocks are?"

One of many versions

Two ministers were scheduled on the Florida Chain of Missions some years ago. They travelled about the state to a series of two-day mission rallies. They were the program for the first morning at each place. For the first four or five rallies they spoke in the same order. At the sixth rally, for some reason the order was reversed and the man who had been speaking second now spoke first. He was a playful sort, apparently. He had heard the other man's speech often enough that he could give it almost verbatim. Which is what he did. Without any explanation he gave the first man's speech.

Without comment, the other speaker gave an entirely different speech. As they got in the car to be taken to the next rally, the speech stealer could wait no longer and inquired if the man noticed that he had given his speech. The man said that he had and he thought he did a good job with it. But he asked further, "But what did you think when you heard me giving your speech?"

"Well," said the other man, "I was surprised, of course. But I had not planned to give that speech here. You must not have known that I came down before the rallies started and gave that speech in this church 10 days ago."

Told me by Bishop John Branscomb

An early Methodist circuit rider was told by his presiding elder: "Never pretend that you know much, or people will soon find out that you are sadly mistaken; neither tell them how little you know, for this they will find out soon enough."

Donald Shelby

The minister was in a dime store. He selected the 50-cent item he had come for only to discover that he had no money with him.

He kiddingly said to the clerk, "Well, I could invite you to hear me preach on Sunday but I am afraid I don't have any 50-cent sermons."

"Perhaps," observed the clerk, "I could come twice."

Then there was the preacher who told a departing woman after worship in which he had preached his first sermon as pastor, "I hope I didn't offend your husband. I saw him leave during my sermon."

She laughed and responded, "Oh, don't pay any attention to him. He has been walking in his sleep since he was a youngster."

The lady said to the preacher, "I am deaf and can't hear a word you say, but I come to church anyhow."

"Maybe you haven't missed much," said the parson humbly.

"Yes," she replied, "that's what they all tell me."

The pastor of the small rural church had died and the job of filling the pulpit fell to the senior deacon. He approached his task with fear but had prepared himself as well as he could.

His first Sunday he handed out paper and pencils to all. Then he said, "We are now going to have a contest. As I preach my lay sermon, I want you to write down every mistake I make. I want you to be very hard on me, don't hold anything back.

At the end of the service I will pick up your papers. And I want to tell you that the one who has the longest list of mistakes wins the grand prize — which is to preach the sermon next Sunday.''

Property

A tourist stopped by to watch a farmer who was erecting a building. He inquired what it was the farmer was building.

"Well," answered the farmer, "if I can rent it, it's a rustic cottage, and if I can't, it's a cow shed."

Q-R

Quakers

A Quaker farmer in Pennsylvania had one cow who was always kicking him and/or the bucket during milking. He had added a special lock to the stanchion and she couldn't move her head. He had attached a gadget to her left leg which was chained to the floor. But it was her right leg that gave the trouble. He milked with the bucket between his knees — harder for her to kick it that way.

One evening she let fly with that leg when he was off balance on the milking stool he used. He fell over backward and the bucket of milk poured all over him. He got up, kicked the bucket across the barn and then went to the front of the stall, unhitched the stanchion, and grabbed the cow by the horns and yanked her head around and looked her eyeball to eyeball (as best he could) and said to her: "Thou art an unruly beast. Thou triest my patience to the extreme. Thou knowest that I am a Quaker and according to my faith, I dare not smite thee. But what thou doest not know is that I can sell thee to that Methodist down the road and he'll whale the tar out of thee!"

H.R.

Reading

A first grader reported to her mother that she found she could read a lot faster if she didn't stop to color the pictures.

Rogers, Will

Some comments by Will Rogers:
"You know horses are smarter than people. You never heard of a horse going broke betting on people."

81

"You know, you've got to exercise your brain just like your muscles."

"One way to solve the traffic problem would be to keep all the cars that are not paid for off the streets. Children could use the streets for playgrounds then."

"I never lack material for my humor column when the Congress is in session."

"Live your life so you wouldn't be afraid to sell the family to the town gossip."

Rules

A farmer was plagued with city folks trespassing on his land without permission. He put up a sign to keep them off. It read: "No Trespassing. Survivors Will Be Prosecuted."

More than 100 years ago the following were Rules at the Mt. Holyoke Seminary for Girls in Massachusetts:

1. No young lady shall become a member of this school who cannot kindle a fire, mash potatoes, or repeat the multiplication table.

2. No cosmetics, perfumeries or fancy soap will be allowed.

3. Every member shall walk a mile a day unless a freshet, an earthquake, or some other calamity prevents.

4. No student shall tarry before the mirror more than three consecutive minutes.

5. No student shall devote more than one hour each week to miscellaneous reading. The *Atlantic Monthly,* Shakespeare, Scott's novels, *Robinson Crusoe,* and immoral works are strictly forbidden. The Bible, the *Boston Recorder, Missionary Herald,* and Washington's Farewell Address are recommended for light reading.

6. No young lady is expected to have gentlemen acquaintances unless they are returned missionaries or agent of some benevolent society.

First heard this in 1939 at Mt. Holyoke

S

Samaritans

A man was driving along a freeway when he noticed a lady by the side of the road trying to change a flat tire on her car. He stopped and offered to help. It was hot and humid, and it was hard and dirty work, but he felt good because he was helping someone who couldn't help herself.

When he finished replacing the tire with the spare, he moved around the car to release the jack, and the woman said to him, "Let the car down easily, please. My husband is asleep in the back seat."

H.R.

Second Coming

A red Porsche convertible pulled up to the red light. Its vanity license had J C on it, the owner's initials. Two nuns were in the next lane and one of them, noticing the license, said, "I knew he was coming back, but I didn't know it would be in a Porsche!"

Sins And Sinner

The painter was supposed to use a quality paint in painting the chancel walls of the church. But he thinned his paint with water. That night he had a dream and the Lord spoke to him and said, "Repaint, you thinner!"

The little boy defined the sins of omission as those which we ought to commit and don't.

83

It was testimony time at the prayer meeting. A man jumped up and shouted, "Brothers and sisters, I have been a miserable and contemptible sinner for years and never knew it before tonight."

A deacon shut him up with, "Sit down Brother. The rest of us have known it for years."

Two young ladies were discussing sin. One confessed that she was jealous of her sister and asked the other, "What is your sin?" The other one replied, "My sin is vanity. I spend hours in front of the mirror admiring my beauty." The first one said, "That's not vanity, dear, that's imagination."

Solomon Wisdom

The seven-year-old was taking care of his two-year-old brother. They were in line at the ice cream stand. The little one shouted loudly that he wanted, "Vanilla, vanilla!" There was no vanilla and some of the parents there watched closely to see how the seven-year-old would handle this crisis. Without hesitation he ordered two strawberry cones. He handed one to his little brother. "Here you are," he said, "pink vanilla."

Sports

St. Peter and Satan were having an argument one day about baseball. With a beguiling leer, Satan proposed a game (to be played on neutral grounds) between a select team from the heavenly host and Satan's own hand-picked team from Hades.

"Very well," the gatekeeper of the Celestial City agreed. "But you realize I hope, Satan, that we have all the good ball players and the best coaches too."

"I know," said Satan calmly, "but we have all the umpires."

"My biggest thrill came the night Elgin Baylor and I combined for 73 points in Madison Square Garden. Elgin had 71 of them." — Hot Rod Hundley

Sports Illustrated

T-U-V

Theology

The late Gerald Kennedy once told about an old lady who heard the implications of evolution explained to her and said, "God grant that it may not be true, but if it is true, God grant that not many people will hear about it."

Tongue Twisters

According to *Guiness Book of Records,* the worst tongue twister is: "The sixth sick sheik's sixth sheep's sick."

Try this: A skunk sat on a stump. The stump thought the skunk stunk, the skunk thought the stump stunk. Which stunk — the stump or the skunk?

T-shirts

"How Can I Fly Like An Eagle When I Have To Work With Turkeys?"

Unexpected Calls

Some years ago Dudley Ward and I were lecturing at a pastor's school in Ocean Grove, New Jersey. Sessions were held in a large parlor of one of the resort hotels on the ocean front. The hotel was equipped with a PA system which had speakers in all the parlors and lobbies and porches of the first floor.

It was an afternoon session and Dr. Ward was lecturing to about 200 Methodist preachers. He became quite personal in what he was saying about how God speaks to persons through the Holy Spirit. He was recalling one memorable experience of his when God was very real to him and he felt God was speaking to him.

"Then," he said, "I was sitting there meditating when all of a sudden I heard the Holy Spirit speaking to me —." At that moment the PA speaker in this parlor buzzed a second and then a voice said, "Calling Dr. Ward, Calling Dr. Ward." If you have ever seen a bunch of preachers crack up, this topped what you saw! In fact, Dudley tried two or three times to start again, but the laughter kept bursting out again. Finally, he gave up and said he would speak about this later, and dismissed us.

H.R.

Viewpoint

Various viewpoints:
His sister: "Oh, his nose is broken!"
His girl: "He can't take me to the dance tonight."
His mother: "Oh, he has lost his front teeth."
His father: "I wonder if the school has insurance."
His coach: "He didn't drop the ball."

Vocabulary (Church Vocabulary Defined)

"Expedite: to compound confusion with commotion."

"Consultant: An ordinary guy who has brass enough to charge 100 times what he is worth."

"To implement a program: Hire more people and expand the budget."

"Committee meeting: a mass mulling of master minds."

"Enrichment process: flooding the discussion with your personal ideas."

"A clarification: to fill in the background with so many details that the foreground goes underground."

"Reliable source: The guy you just met."

"Unimpeachable source: The guy who started the original rumor."

"Mission strategy: First get the money and then we will decide what to do with it."

W

Weather

A property survey was made of an old lady's property which was near the border. Decisions had to be made whether it was in Canada or the U.S. The official announced to her that her property was just inside the U.S. She seemed relieved and said, "I'm so glad to know that. They say that Canadian winters are much more severe than those in the U.S.

Wishes

Rocky Bleier, when he was a balding Pittsburgh Steeler running back, expressed his wishes: "I'd like the body of Jim Brown, the moves of Gayle Sayers, the strength of Earl Campbell, and the acceleration of O.J. Simpson. And just once I would like to run and feel the wind in my hair."

Words

My college professor said there is a two word sentence which embodies every basic grammatical error. It is "Them's them."

H.R.

Some more linguistic obfuscation:
"Automotive internist" — garage mechanic
"Activity booster" — Pep pills
"Early learning centers" — preschool

"Pupil stations" — desks
"Instructional resource center" — library
"Volume variances from plan" — Litton Industries words for a strike
"Strategic withdrawal" — retreat
"A phased withdrawal" — a route with insufficient transport

Collected from various sources

World Problems

The guy had been shipwrecked years before and had lived alone on this desert island. One day he was excited to see a ship off-shore which had seen his signal flag in the palm tree. A small dinghy came ashore with one occupant. The fellow rowing it handed the marooned sailor a bundle of newspapers and told him, "The captain sends you these papers and suggests you read them before you decide whether you want to be rescued."

Acknowledgments

Books

Abingdon Press for permission to quote from:
Choose To Win, Ernest G. Schmidt, to whom the rights reverted.

The Master Book Of Humorous Illustrations, by Leewin Williams. Renewal 1966 by Chester M. Williams.

The Happy Clergy, compiled by Herb Walker, copyright 1977.

Permission from Mrs. J. Wallace Hamilton, to whom rights have reverted for quotations from books by J. Wallace Hamilton, including:
Who Goes There? Copyright Fleming Revel Co., 1958.

The Thunder Of Bare Feet, Copyright Fleming Revel Co., 1954.

Serendipity, Copyright Fleming Revel Co., 1955.

Where Now Is Thy God? Copyright Fleming Revel Co., 1969.

Permission is granted from Harper and Row, Publishers, Inc., New York, New York, for quotations from *Fresh Every Morning by* Gerald Kennedy.

Periodicals

The Atlanta Constitution, Atlanta, Georgia, for selections from its columnist Leo Aikman.

Cappers for selections from "Storyteller's Column."

The Christian Century, Chicago, Illinois.

The Clergy Journal, Copyright 1980, by Church Management Inc., Austin, Texas 78716, for selections by C. Thomas Hilton, October, 1980, page 10.

Clergy Talk, published without copyright by Tomlinson Publishing Co., Sequim, Washington 98382, as a service to the clergy through Funeral Home distribution.

Context, edited by Martin Martin, for three selections.

The Detroit Free Press, Detroit, Michigan, for selections from its columnists Joe Fall and Bob Talbert.

Grit, Michael A. Rafferty, Williamsport, Pennsylvania, for several selections.

The Lion Magazine, published by Lions International, Oak Brook, Illinois, for selections from the "Laugh" page in several issues.

The New American, formerly *American Opinion,* Appleton, Wisconsin 54913, F.R. Duplantier, editor, for selections from various issues.

Quote, published without copyright in Slidel, Louisiana 70549, selections from weekly issues from 1950-1983, with credit to original source or individual where indicated.

Sports Illustrated, Time Inc., Magazines, New York, New York, excerpts from various issues.

Individuals

The following ministers with whom I exchange sermon reprints have given permission for the use of various stories from their sermons:

Barry Bailey, Fort Worth, Texas; Raymond F. Balcomb, Portland, Oregon; C. Rex Bevins, Lincoln, Nebraska; Thomas L. Butts, Fort Walton Beach, Florida; Clarence Forsberg, Columbia, Missouri; Donald J. Shelby, Santa Monica, California; Mark Trotter, San Diego, California; Melvin E. Wheatley, Denver, Colorado; Rodney E. Wilmoth, Omaha, Nebraska.

Other ministers and laypersons who have contributed stories include: Tom H. Matheny, Hammond, Louisiana; Donald Miller, Gaithersburg, Maryland; and Wilson Weldon, Lake Junaluska, North Carolina.

Deceased clergy friends and colleagues who are sources for stories include: Rev. Lynn H. Rupert, Bishop Paul. B. Kern and Bishop John Branscomb.

To all these publishers and persons I express sincere gratitude.

Index